Which way to God?

EVANGELICAL PRESS

EVANGELICAL PRESS
Faverdale North, Darlington, DL3 OPH, England

Evangelical Press USA
P. O. Box 84, Auburn, MA 01501, USA

e-mail: sales@evangelical-press.org
web: www.evangelical-press.org

First published 2000

British Library Cataloguing in Publication Data available

ISBN 0 85234 413 9

Printed in Singapore by SNP Printing Pte Ltd

Questions
Questions
Questions ...

Life can be very confusing. You have to make decisions and sometimes feel unqualified to do so. You wouldn't set out on a journey without knowing where you were going or how to get there. You would find a map. You would ask for directions. You must know the way. You have opened this book to find your way to God. But which way is the right way? Lack of information, conflicting advice, and plain ignorance, can leave you bewildered in the face of the choices available.

So many religions

Most religions claim to point people to God. Therefore we must take care when searching for God and considering the source of life and its purpose. There are so many religions and so many different teachings about God that this is no simple task.

Some think it is easy. They say it is just like choosing goods from a supermarket shelf. 'You have all these brands to choose from,' they say, 'so just take the one that suits you! After all, they are all much the same, aren't they? I like Jesus, you like Allah, someone else likes Buddha — it doesn't really make any difference.' But are they right?

Do all religions lead to God?

Most people think that they do, but that would mean that religious teachings that completely contradict each other are all true. This clearly cannot be so! We would never accept such a thing in any other area of life, so why accept it when it comes to the question of God?

So which one is right? Let us ask four basic questions:

Who is God?
What is man?
What is sin?
Who is Jesus Christ?

These questions are not merely a matter of debate or curiosity. They are essential in understanding what life is all about. You will find answers to these questions as you read on.

Who is God?

— Does anyone know?

This is probably one of the oldest questions ever asked, and it demands an answer! Believing in a Supreme Being and yet never truly knowing who such a being is seems as futile as believing in happiness and never wishing to experience it.

Where do we find the answer?

Some say that there is no answer because there is no God. Others say there may be a God but it is impossible for us to know him, so again the question cannot be answered. But most people believe that there is a God, a Supreme Being of some sort. Their problem is that although they accept that God exists, they know nothing about him.

So who is he? What is he like? How can we know him? Sadly, the answers people give reveal more about themselves than they do about God. Asked what he thought God was like, a famous sportsman replied, 'An old man with a beard sitting on a cloud.' In voicing this opinion, he was reflecting the views of many people.

What has God said about himself?
It is no use asking others for answers to these questions. They, too, are just as likely to be confused. You must look instead at what God has told us about himself. Where can you find this information? The answer is in the Bible. There, God has provided answers for anyone who seriously wants to know him. They may not be the answers you expect, but they are God's answers, which is why the Bible often refers to itself as the 'Word of God'.

There we find that God is gloriously and wonderfully unique.[1] There never was a time when God did not exist,[2] for he created time and space and everything in them. If there had been no God, there would have been no universe, no world. [3]

God is not like anyone or anything else
The Bible warns us against making up our own ideas about God. Speaking through the prophets, God declares, 'To whom will you compare me? Or who is my equal?'[4] 'You thought I was altogether like you,'[5] but 'My ways [are] higher than your ways and my thoughts than your thoughts.'[6]

The Bible shows us a God who is unique, unchanging and ever-present.[7] The greatest thing it tells us about God is that he is holy.[8] Because he is holy he will not, and cannot, tolerate any sin in us. That, as we shall see, creates an immense problem for each one of us.

What is man?

If the question, 'Who is God?' has perplexed people for centuries, so too has the question: 'What is man?' This is particularly true in our day and age. With all our knowledge and scientific progress, people are still not happy or satisfied. We may understand things today that baffled our forefathers, but we still cannot understand ourselves.

Are men and women only animals?

If there is no God, then man is only an animal, a physical being. This is a popular view today. We are told that mankind is the product of a mindless process of evolution. If this is so, our greatest needs are physical and material. Such things as prosperity and pleasure are all that matter. If there is no God, then we should 'eat, drink and be merry, for tomorrow we die'. If there is no God, then life has little meaning, and right and wrong are simply what we like or dislike.

We are spiritual beings

But the Bible presents an altogether different (and more logical) picture. Man is a being made by God, for God and in the image of God.[9] This does not mean a physical image; it means that you, like God, have a moral and rational nature — you can reason, design, worship and explore like no other of God's creations. You also have a conscience that tells you the difference between right and wrong, though at times you may ignore it.

The most important issue

Your need is that nothing should stand between you and God. Material problems, though not to be ignored, are no longer the main issue. The most important thing is to be right with God.

If there is a God, then death is not the end, and you will only find a purpose in life when you seek him. To be accepted by God becomes of prime importance. Unlike all other creatures in this world, man alone can know God.

But if man is so privileged, why does he do so much evil?
Why all the killings and murders?
Why so much hatred and bitterness?
Why wars and hostility?
Why are we destroying the environment?

Why, in a world of plenty, do so many die of starvation?

Why…? Why…? Why…?

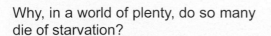

The basic answer to these questions is that something called 'sin' has shattered the image of God in man and destroyed our knowledge of our Maker. What, then, is sin?

What is sin?

The essence of sin is to fall short of what God requires of us. The Bible says that we are all sinners.[10] Because there is sin in our hearts, we deliberately go against what God says we should do, wanting our way rather than his. Indeed, our whole lives are ones of rebellion against God. Sin is part of our very nature.

Is sin a serious problem?
There are people today foolish enough to think that sin doesn't matter. We should 'live and let live', they say. So sin is made the focus of entertainment; it is played with, applauded and generally looked upon as harmless.

Sin is like a cancer
Crime, cruelty and vice are only its more extreme symptoms. Sin is seen first in disregard for God, and then spreads to a lack of concern for others. It emerges in the selfishness and greed of ordinary people, and in the breakdown of family life. By our sin, we all contribute to the mess the world is in, and we all suffer because of it. But there is even worse news.

Sin creates an unbridgeable gap
God holds us accountable for the way we live our lives. He does not turn a blind eye to our sins, as many think. The Lord Jesus Christ said, 'I tell you that men will have to give account on the day of judgement for every careless word they have spoken.'[11] If we are to answer to God for every thoughtless word, what of our bad thoughts and selfish actions?

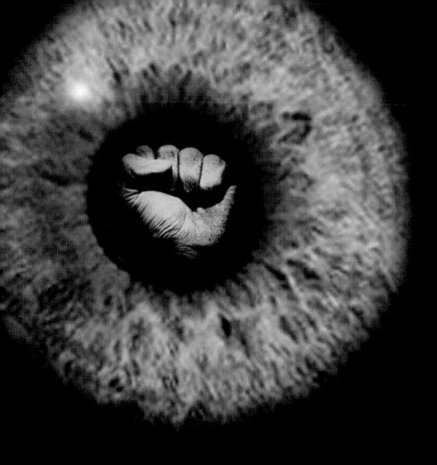

Your sin and rebellion against God have created an unbridgeable gap between God and you. The Bible says that, spiritually, you are 'dead' because of your sins.[12] You can do nothing to bridge the gap between you and a perfectly holy God who cannot tolerate sin. This is the barrier, the blockade, running between you and God. It is one that you cannot dismiss or break down. How, then, will it be overcome? How can God be approached peacefully? The answer lies in the Lord Jesus Christ.

The basic problem is that people do not take God seriously. Therefore, they do not take sin seriously. To them, sin is just a social blemish or a moral hiccup. So if they think about salvation at all, it is always in terms of what they can do, by moral or religious effort, to improve their life. That is what the Bible calls trying to obtain 'salvation by works'.

Man's way does not work!

It seems so reasonable and plausible. If I have a problem with sin, I must pull myself together, turn over a new leaf and change my ways. It sounds good, but it does not work. Our problem lies in our fallen nature — what we are — and no amount of tinkering with morality or religion can change that nature.[13]

Man's way — the wrong way

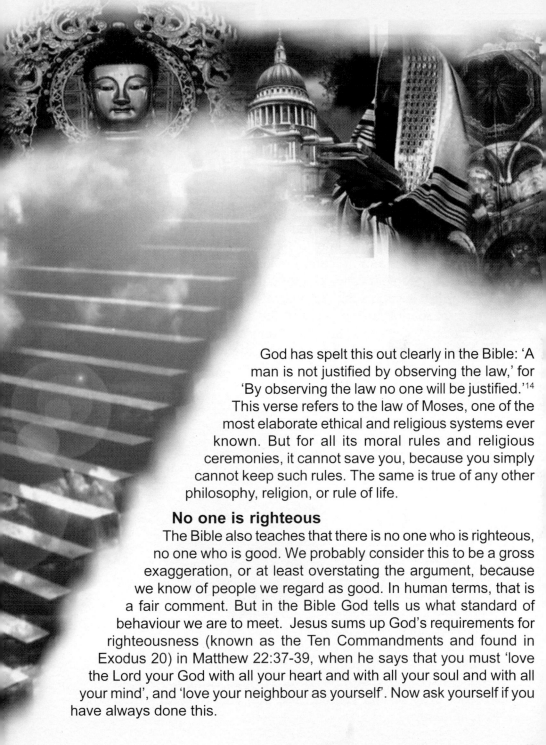

God has spelt this out clearly in the Bible: 'A man is not justified by observing the law,' for 'By observing the law no one will be justified.'[14] This verse refers to the law of Moses, one of the most elaborate ethical and religious systems ever known. But for all its moral rules and religious ceremonies, it cannot save you, because you simply cannot keep such rules. The same is true of any other philosophy, religion, or rule of life.

No one is righteous

The Bible also teaches that there is no one who is righteous, no one who is good. We probably consider this to be a gross exaggeration, or at least overstating the argument, because we know of people we regard as good. In human terms, that is a fair comment. But in the Bible God tells us what standard of behaviour we are to meet. Jesus sums up God's requirements for righteousness (known as the Ten Commandments and found in Exodus 20) in Matthew 22:37-39, when he says that you must 'love the Lord your God with all your heart and with all your soul and with all your mind', and 'love your neighbour as yourself'. Now ask yourself if you have always done this.

No one has kept God's law

The honest answer is that you have not kept God's law. No one is so perfect as to be acceptable to God. In your heart of hearts you know that this is true, because God has given each of us a conscience.[15] Both conscience and the Bible tell us we are sinners. No matter how hard you try, you cannot reach the standard that God has set.

Why can't you keep God's laws?

The New Testament explanation is that 'the god of this age' (the devil) has blinded people's minds so that they cannot believe.[16] The result is that man, by nature, cannot understand things that relate to God, 'For they are foolishness to him, and he cannot understand them, because they are spiritually discerned.'[17]

When you think about this seriously, it is just about the only reasonable explanation. If the God who made us says categorically, 'You cannot save yourselves,' and you reply that you can, that is more than arrogance or stupidity; it is spiritual blindness.

Physical blindness is a great affliction. The colour of the sunset, or the grandeur of a mountain range, even the smile on a loved one's face, are lost on those who lack the gift of sight.

Your greatest need

So it is with spiritual blindness. Spiritual reality is there, but you cannot comprehend it. Perhaps even as you read this, this talk of God, sin, salvation, eternity, and so on, makes no sense to you.

Your great need, therefore, is for spiritual sight, for God to open your eyes so that you can see with your mind and trust with your heart.

There is a way that seems right

Many people have difficulty with the idea that Jesus Christ is the unique and exclusive way to God. They think that such claims are bigoted and intolerant. Surely, they say, there must be many ways that people can come to God.

Is sincerity enough?

They picture life as a mountain, with many paths leading to its summit. God is on the mountain peak, and it does not matter which path people take — the Christian path, the Moslem path, the Hindu path, or even the atheist path — all will eventually lead to God as long as people are sincere.

A wise man once wrote, 'There is a way that seems right to a man, but in the end it leads to death.'[18] By 'way' this Bible verse means the path a person takes through life — your beliefs, behaviour, attitudes and concerns.

Where does the way go?

The most important thing about a way is where it goes. The person who chooses a way of life without knowing where it leads is, says the Bible, a fool.[19]

But the words 'seem right' suggest a degree of sincerity. You may not deliberately be going the wrong way. You may see no harm or danger in your chosen path. It seems all right. Surely you cannot be blamed if you do what you think is right?

Ignoring what God has said

God says you can and will be blamed, in spite of your sincerity, if you choose to ignore his warnings and the gospel's call to repent from your sin and believe in Jesus Christ.

You can be blamed, particularly, because Jesus has warned us clearly that there are two 'ways' with very different destinations.

We like to think there are many choices open to us in life. In one sense, that is true. We can choose a career, where to live, whom to marry, what to do with our money, and many other things. These choices will dictate the way we live.

But Jesus said that, fundamentally, there are only two ways: 'Enter through the narrow gate. For wide is the gate and broad is the road that leads to destruction, and many enter through it. But small is the gate and narrow the road that leads to life, and only a few find it.'[20]

There are only two ways — man's way that has no time for Christ, and God's way that is Christ.

God's answer — the right way

Think of it like this. Some restaurants insist on a certain standard of dress, and refuse to allow a man in if he is not wearing a tie. Customers may object, but the proprietors have a perfect right to maintain their standards.

There is a standard to be met

However, as businessmen, they do not want to turn customers away. So when a man is refused admission, they will then say, 'Don't go away, sir. We will provide you with a tie!' Once this is provided and put on, the standard is met and there is no barrier to admission. The restaurant has set its standard, but then provides its own answer for those who fall short of it.

Jesus gives a similar illustration. A man was found at a wedding not wearing the special garment provided for him (and every other guest) by the host. Because he did not meet the dress-standard required, and refused to accept the host's provision, he was thrown out.[21]

Perfect righteousness

Perfect righteousness is the standard God has set for entry to his presence. No one who sins will be allowed to know him or enter heaven. That effectively bars us all.

But the gospel (the 'good news') is that God has met his own requirement, and provides the perfect 'garment' for us, namely, the righteousness of Christ.[22]

Saved by grace through faith

God, in his Word, says that salvation is by grace through faith in Jesus Christ.[23] The word 'salvation' means different things to different people. To some it refers to being rescued from things like alcoholism or drug abuse. For others it means economic or social deliverance, like being saved from poverty and deprivation. But when the Bible speaks of being 'saved' it means to be delivered from the guilt and punishment that your sin deserves, and from its ruling power in your heart.

This salvation is offered to you as a free gift from God — by grace. You do not deserve it. You do not have to pay for it. You do not have to earn it.

Faith is also a gift from God. It is the channel by which this grace comes to you as you repent from your sins and look to Jesus Christ alone for salvation.[24] Whereas before you were spiritually blind, now, through faith, you are given spiritual eyesight. All these things now make sense to you! Faith sees no hope of ever earning salvation, but every hope of receiving it as a gift. Through faith, you acknowledge that you are a sinner and that you need a saviour. This is God's way of salvation.

Who is Jesus Christ?

Jesus of Nazareth lived in Palestine two thousand years ago. Our calendar is reckoned from the time of his birth, which many celebrate around the world at Christmas. His life story and teaching are recorded in the four 'Gospels' in the New Testament. But there are also many prophecies in the Old Testament, written hundreds of years before his birth, which were fulfilled in detail by his life and death.

The prophecies tell us, for example, that Christ would be born of a virgin[25] in Bethlehem,[26] that he would ride into Jerusalem on a donkey[27] and be betrayed for thirty pieces of silver.[28] Jesus himself said he would be killed but would rise again on the third day.[29]

Remarkable claims

The Bible makes many remarkable claims about Jesus. It says that he is the Son of God (John 3:18). He is also God (John 1:1). He is sinless (Hebrews 4:15). He perfomed miracles (Matthew 14:13-36). He raised the dead to life (John 11). He himself rose from the dead (Matthew 28:6).

In fact the entire Bible is about the Lord Jesus Christ, who he is, what he has done and what he is going to do.[30] The people who lived with Jesus, and observed his life at close quarters, took his claims very seriously. Otherwise, they would not have recorded his teaching and miracles as sober truth, as they did in the New Testament writings. It is interesting that modern man so easily dismisses both Jesus and the New Testament as mythological. Yet those who saw what Jesus did and heard what he taught were willing to die for him.

The only way

We began this booklet by asking if different religions are simply different paths to the same God. The Bible's answer is: 'No, Jesus is unique.' He himself claimed to be the only way to God. He said, 'I am the way and the truth and the life. No one comes to the Father except through me.'[31]

A way back to God

The good news (the 'gospel') is that when Jesus Christ died on the cross, 'he bore the sin of many'[32] and saved them from God's anger against sin and the judgement they deserve.

He alone was innocent of sin and could act as a substitute — he stood in our place and took the punishment his people deserved. He died, 'the righteous for the unrighteous, to bring you to God'.[33] By his death he not only turns away God's anger, but also reconciles to God all that the Father has given him.[34]

Jesus is God's way of salvation, which is why he is the only way.

Jesus is the way

Jesus is no ordinary person. He is God become man. He left heaven to seek and save the lost.

When Jesus came to earth in Bethlehem at the first Christmas, angels thrilled at the salvation he was bringing and sang his praises. Thirty-three years later when Jesus died on the cross there were no angels singing. They must have been amazed when they realized what the cost of man's salvation was to be. Perhaps they said to God, 'Not him for them! Not the holy, sinless Jesus for the hell-deserving rebels that all men and women are!' But that was God's way.

God's love

God loved us so much that he sent Jesus to be our substitute,[35] to take our punishment and to die instead of us, so that 'To all who received him, to those who believed in his name, he gave the right to become children of God.'[36]

Jesus died for sinners

Jesus died an agonizing death on a Roman cross. But his greatest suffering did not lie in the physical pain, but in the condemnation he endured from God the Father, as he bore all the sins of his people. On the cross, 'God made him who had no sin to be sin for us, so that in him we might become the righteousness of God.'[37]

The cross was God's supreme act of love and grace. At the cross we see God, in all his divine holiness, dealing with human sin. At the cross, God removed the sin that separates his people from him by making his Son, the Lord Jesus, responsible for guilty sinners' violations of divine law. At the cross, God credits our sin and guilt to Jesus, while crediting Jesus' righteousness to us. At the cross God's wrath fell upon his Son instead of us.

Jesus satisfies all of God's requirements

Sin is punished as God prescribed that it should be. There is now nothing further that divine justice can demand because Jesus has paid the debt in full.

Jesus is the only way because he alone is the way that God has provided for us. The Bible says of Jesus Christ that 'Salvation is found in no one else, for there is no other name under heaven given to men by which we must be saved.'[38]

Jesus now says to you, 'Come to me, all you who are weary and burdened, and I will give you rest'[39] — he will deal with your sin and make you acceptable to God.

You come by realizing that you are guilty and that you do not deserve pardon. But pardon is what you need. To 'come' means to believe in Jesus as God's only answer to deal with your sin and to provide pardon for guilty sinners. It means to trust what he did on your behalf on the cross and to look to him alone for forgiveness and salvation.

Becoming a Christian

If you are serious about becoming a Christian, there are a few things you need to understand.

Becoming a Christian is not like joining a club; neither is it the same as taking up a new interest or hobby. Your desire to be a Christian has to become an overwhelming necessity. Such a desire will not be created by a casual interest, but only by God working in your heart and mind.

You cannot make yourself a Christian

You may decide to call yourself a Christian, but that is not the same as actually being one. This is because of what a Christian is.

By definition a Christian is a 'Christ-person', one who loves the Lord Jesus Christ and seeks to live his or her life according to the Saviour's teachings. But this is contrary to all that you are by nature, so to become a Christian your nature must be changed. Only God can do that.

God must change you

In the Bible, we are told that Christians are 'God's workmanship'.[40] Each Christian is the product of an extraordinary work of the Spirit of Almighty God.

Does this mean that there is nothing that you should do, and that you must just wait for God to work in you? Not at all.

The Bible says that you must respond to the good news about Jesus Christ. The prophet Isaiah wrote:

Seek the Lord while he may be found;
    call on him while he is near.
Let the wicked forsake his way
    and the evil man his thoughts.
Let him turn to the Lord, and he will have mercy on him,
    and to our God, for he will freely pardon.[41]

These verses say three things:

1. You must seek God while there is still time

How? God can and must be 'found'. Looking for God is the most important thing that you will ever do. Read the Bible, 'call upon him' in prayer. He 'is near'.

2. You must repent

These verses emphasize the need to repent. Repenting means that you accept that your ways are evil in the sight of God. It means acknowledging that you stand condemned before a holy God and that you need to turn to him as the only way. It means turning away from your sin and rejection of God.[42] It is a complete change of life and direction. Only God can help you do this. The Bible calls it being born again.[43]

3. You must turn to God

These verses command you to turn to God in the expectation that he will forgive and receive you. This you do by believing in the Lord Jesus Christ as the one who justifies the ungodly through his death and resurrection. You must believe that God exists,[44] that he sent his Son to die for your sins and that he can and will save you, if you turn to him in repentance and faith.[45] When you turn to God, you can rely on what the Lord Jesus has said, that 'All that the Father gives me will come to me, and whoever comes to me I will never drive away.'[46]

Which way?

The writer was at a meeting one Saturday night in Bristol. The hall was packed, and after the meeting the crowd spilled out onto the road as they made their way to their cars and coaches. At the same time, thousands more were leaving cinemas and theatres. The roads were jammed solid with traffic. Nothing was moving.

We were parked in a multi-storey car park behind the hall, on the fifth floor of the eleven-storey building. All the ramps leading down to the road were blocked with cars bumper to bumper. I thought we would never get out.

But a friend who was with me, and knew Bristol well, advised us not to go down, as everyone else was doing, but to go up. This was hard advice to swallow. How can you get out of a multi-storey car park by going up?

But there was nothing to lose, so we followed his advice. Everyone else was going down; we alone were going up.

And there, incredibly, was a way out on the eighth floor! The car park was built against the side of a hill and the eighth floor provided an exit to the top of the hill behind.

The obvious way out was down, but my friend knew another and better way. Life is full of frustrations and difficulties, and men and women are looking for answers. But man's answers only sink us deeper in the mire. There is another way, and that way is Jesus Christ.

Which way are you taking?

R e f e r e n c e s

1.	Isaiah 46:9	24.	Hebrews 11:1; Romans 5:1-2
2.	Psalm 90:2; John 17:5	25.	Isaiah 7:14
3.	Revelation 4:11	26.	Micah 5:2
4.	Isaiah 40:25	27.	Zechariah 9:9
5.	Psalm 50:21	28.	Zechariah 11:12
6.	Isaiah 55:9	29.	Matthew 20:19
7.	Isaiah 45:21; Malachi 3:6; Psalm 139:7-10	30.	Luke 24:27
8.	Exodus 15:11	31.	John 14:6
9.	Genesis 1:27	32.	Isaiah 53:12
10.	Romans 3:23	33.	1 Peter 3:18
11.	Matthew 12:36	34.	2 Timothy 1:9-10; John 17:2
12.	Ephesians 2:1	35.	John 3:16
13.	Romans 8:7-8	36.	John 1:12
14.	Galatians 2:16	37.	2 Corinthians 5:21
15.	Romans 2:12-16	38.	Acts 4:12
16.	2 Corinthians 4:4	39.	Matthew 11:28
17.	1 Corinthians 2:14	40.	Ephesians 2:10
18.	Proverbs 14:12	41.	Isaiah 55:6-7
19.	Luke 12:16-21	42.	Acts 20:21
20.	Matthew 7:13-14	43.	John 3:3
21.	Matthew 22:11-14	44.	Hebrews 11:6
22.	Romans 3:22	45.	Acts 16:31; John 3:16
23.	Ephesians 2:8	46.	John 6:37